T0149195

THE
GLORY
SHALL
BE
REVEALED

WAYNE
CONNOR

authorHOUSE®

AuthorHouse™
1663 Liberty Drive
Bloomington, IN 47403
www.authorhouse.com
Phone: 1 (800) 839-8640

© 2017 Wayne Connor. All rights reserved.

No part of this book may be reproduced, stored in a retrieval system, or transmitted by any means without the written permission of the author.

Published by AuthorHouse 06/13/2017

ISBN: 978-1-5246-9559-0 (sc)
ISBN: 978-1-5246-9558-3 (hc)
ISBN: 978-1-5246-9569-9 (e)

Library of Congress Control Number: 2017908943

Print information available on the last page.

Any people depicted in stock imagery provided by Thinkstock are models, and such images are being used for illustrative purposes only. Certain stock imagery © Thinkstock.

This book is printed on acid-free paper.

Because of the dynamic nature of the Internet, any web addresses or links contained in this book may have changed since publication and may no longer be valid. The views expressed in this work are solely those of the author and do not necessarily reflect the views of the publisher, and the publisher hereby disclaims any responsibility for them.

CONTENTS

A HUSH

A hush comes over me as I look at you.
I could hear no other sound save the pounding of my heart.
There before me, is a goddess with eyes a brown or blue.
Who shines with a grace and beauty denied any work of art.

A hush muffles my heart when you smile.
I instantly know you possess a heavenly quality, which mortal women lack.
Not just beautiful, your face has a radiance which has no guile.
And you hair, like streams of a dark void flowing down your back.

A hush comes over my soul as you walk towards me,
Approaching is a celestial being, i begin to doubt my sanity.
You have to be a goddess queen, from mythology.
Because no mortal woman, holds such beauty.

A hush is the only noise, the only verse.
A brief kiss and then you outstretch your beautiful hand.
Silence still reigns, but now i do understand.
I must follow you queen, or forever have my mind afflicted with you,
Like a curse.

PROPHECY OF BEAUTY AND DEATH

Fulfillment of a ten thousand year old prophecy.
Earth itself seems to have an irregular turn.
When the earth is graced with the perfect beauty.
Next day, that same earth must burn.

This is not divine prophecy, but a man-made yarn.
Or so down the millennia it was thought.
Many took the message to encourage, not to warn,
Of an overwhelming beauty juggernaut.

I hear of a rash spread of blind then dead men.
The blind, blame their ensuing death, from seeing a walking
vision.
They say she is something beyond mortal imagination.
Even more than a vision, she is a walking heaven.

To see her would supposedly cost me my life.
Tomorrow the world should burn anyway.
But I the chosen, could certainly make thing right.
Then not just man, but the earth won't pass away.

The moon is bright as sunlight at midnight.
I lose sight as over the bloody plains she came.
As seconds tick away, I begin to feel death's bite.
At a minute past twelve, the entire planet burns in her
flames.

THE TAINT

I am light and i am dark.
The light is surrounded
By darkness.
Within the ebony, there is a consistent spark.
To keep the temple, from
Slipping into madness.

Weaker innocents are
Engulfed by pure ebon.
Flames tainted by black crimson.
These souls are more often
Lost than won.
If they don't snatch hold
To the risen Son.

All are chosen, because
All have been given free will.
How can love be greatest to a
Heart that's frozen?
How can the Son overcome a
Nature that wants the thrill
And the kill?

The flesh is the darkness.
The soul is the light.
Charity or love; the greatest
Gift is this.
What does it mean in the presence of such a colossal fight?

Ever lurking, is sin and death.
Always hoping to catch someone with
The taint, when they breath their last breath.
The chosen must strengthen their light,
With the son of righteousness.
Or the taint will give a cold caress.

And be the first to welcome you to hell.
The flesh or the darkness, conquers very well.
With the aid of sin and death,
The taint is almost invincible.
Unless, the chosen choose the Son.
Then let their hearts be made whole.
And also their soul.

BETRAYERS

Smile, smile, smile.
All times their minds filled with guile.
Flawless, masked expressions.
Only to other betrayers,
They make their demonic confessions.

Humanity long gone.
Just a decaying soul left,
To sing grave songs.
Even their cologne has the stench of death.

Pale ghastly links to a dragon's chain.
Iconoclast of sins, twist purity to pain.
Addiction to a level that they betray themselves.
And decorate their homes with sepulchers as shelves.

Mind numbing stupidity,
Dressed up as intelligence.
Bits of pieces of decency,
Give the betrayers a faint presence.

ABYSS ECLIPSES

Abyss eclipses overwhelm a gasping heart.
Tides terribly turn and rip the soul's core apart.
Startling revelations to a soul dubbed invincible
Unaccustomed urges surge for the gasping heart to make it full.
He stumbles towards the inevitable collapse.
Only mere unaccustomed urges on which to grasp.
Defiant shell tenses and rise to one knee.
While gasping heart and soul's core beckon him to flee.
Tears rush and cuddle his shattered being.
Words boldly come to give unaccustomed urges meaning.
"Marry me my love", is what the words did blurt.
To she who seemed like a goddess visiting humble earth.
Time paused, as eternity waited for an answer.
Lulls in nothingness felt like a thousand cancers.
Huge questions of being damned or feeling blessed.
Eternity gasped as all eclipses were forever moved with a yes.

MADNESS

Lunacy, tea for two and me.
Warped pain preferred than ecstasy.
Fleetly flee off into December's eve.
Rabid ravings, now all the senses leave.

What good is a utopia consumed by lava?
Sail and ride the wind to Java.
Mortals given presents, which are their lives.
Kings treated as peasants, and ruled by their wives.

Only a design.
All emotions resign,
Dreams and reality intertwine.
And fire with crystalline.

The sane now twisted.
Insanity now enlisted.
Logic now resisted,
And craziness now insisted.

Thoughts of power to a point of being demented.
Madness eternal in the mind cemented.
Self-proclaimed counselors deduce by wits,
And start to get glad.
But no human can fully describe a mind gone mad.

MADNESS REVISITED

Cracks in consciousness,
Finds fusion in fantasies.
Ashes and anomalies,
Binds blightful black bliss.

Madness masked with sanity.
Ten years without loss of one step.
All knowledge needs to be more in depth,
As vampire vixens vaunt vague vanity.

Cryptic conclusions.
Shadowy solutions.
Iconoclastic illusions, includes
Cold contusions.

A mind mad for many years,
Feels no more pain.
Yet, it can instantly summon tears,
To hide the fact about being insane.

It is sad really,
To see a woman adorned with black lilies.
To see a perfect person, who made the perfect filly.
Shift with symbiosis and change the name to billy.

Kings no more subject to peasants.
Clever ruses have always been run through.
Death of the devils made them feel pleasant.

Birth of the angels, made them like birds coo.

New, stronger castles inside tower.
Nothing can make God inquisitive.
He gave the author wisdom with his infinite power.
He from the dawn of time knew, madness would be revisited.

CERTAINLY

Across a crowded room, our eyes did meet.
Like a scene recalled from an ancient fairy tale.
The high caliber pace of my heart was indiscreet.
Because you seemed to be a gift, an angel had unveiled.
Of course, you must be an angel walking among men.
The beauty you possess, makes me only think of heaven.
Certainly, the prettiest of all women you seem,
Or certainly a mystic, mesmerizing like a controller of dreams.
Certainly, to the atheist you must odd, because
Certainly, you are the proof there is a supreme God.

ALONE AND LONELY

A sadness if only to comprehend.
A person going through life without a friend.
Wounded, wearily wondering within their own world.
Crying, cold and complacent, and in a corner curled.
Acquaintances, they haven't seen in years,
They still consider close companions.
No one there, to share the cheers, or wipe the tears,
When something good or bad happens.
A diverse existence for the alone and lonely.
Often living in dreams, than living in reality.
What they say is true, many might consider fantasy.
Not really sure, if living a life of solitude,
Isn't living a life of insanity.
The only thing celebrated at birthdays or holidays,
Is there own heartbeat.
When they venture into society the hurt isn't displayed.
Their facade seems so trendy and so sweet.
Yet, pride and monotony, allows the rouse to continue.
Loneliness so well masked, even the lonely believe their own
Lies are true.
Until a scene of a man and woman, strips
And skewers the facade off and through.
The sight of the couple, left what's left of a heart, open for
public view.
Tears tears tears.
Pain pain pain.
Visions of so many lost and lonely years.
Consistently fret and fatigue a lonely person's brain.

Alone and lonely, what a sad state for anybody.
Alone and lonely, with tears your only company.
Alone and lonely, what a sad state for you to be.
Alone and lonely, alone and lonely.

WITH ALONE AGAIN

He finds himself with alone again,
He thought that demon had been banished.
For alone he started having sympathy pains,
So he knew for him only alone had been famished.

Coldness in the barren fields of his heart.
Overwhelming forces he forced to run away.
Most have sneaked back, hoping to have a fresh start.
Only divine help can completely keep those forces at bay.

Relationships replaced by ghost towns.
Memories are all that remain.
Open smiles, turned to masked frowns,
And dreams are allowed, but only if they are insane.

A frigid phoenix reborn beside his life,
That never takes the usual 500 years.
Alone is reborn when there are images of a future wife.
Alone is reborn, when his face becomes stained with tears.

Seasons changed to an eternal winter.
It's like a legendary spell from mythology.
One touch from alone, caused his heart to split and splinter.
Then make the last of his emotions flee.
Memories transformed into despair.
Callouses form on his very soul
No one else does, so he doesn't care.
Next, his heart turned into a black hole.

An entire life engulfed by sadness.
God himself was begged to exile the pain.
Now leaves the cold, and in comes gladness.
God is with him, so he won't be with alone again.

ALONE AS A WOUNDED TIGER

Alone as a wounded tiger, he walks the earth.

On the prowl, cautiously stepping, searching and stalking.

He was injured, stabbed in the back by one who started to hunt with him.

This betrayer left him for dead, but he arose with an unrivalled rage, a blinding fury to

Destroy this deceiver of friends.

Like a passing thought the foe was ripped, shredded to pieces.

Feeble attempts to open a new wound ended in a terrible demise.

The wound he has, cannot, and will not heal.

Now he is different from other tigers.

They hunt because they have to. He now believes those who do not hunt will

Be hunted.

Alone as a wounded tiger, he roams in a familiar darkness.

The only thing to watch his back is the shadows.

Pain, the horrible pain; a clap of thunder can be heard as he roars in defiance of this dreaded

Hurt.

He realizes the suffering will be with him from now to the end of his eternity.

The more anguish he feels, the stronger he becomes.

It is like a supply of food fed to some poor soul dying of starvation.

Alone as a wounded tiger he will go on a journey, or embark on an unknown quest.

Others try to prove their loyalty to this true king of beasts, but rather prove their betraying habits.

He would rather hunt as an individual, alone as a wounded tiger.

The wound is far deeper than his flesh.

It is in his heart!

There, the wound seems to be tearing at this tough blood pump.

Pulling at the very center of it.

From this wound emotions flow free.

Soon, all of his emotions will be gone.

At that moment he will cease to exist.

By an act of God, he realizes that his wound must be mended.

He now knows, the reason for his journey.

He is trying to find another; one he can trust to talk, walk, and stalk with him.

Alone as a Wounded Tiger he still hunts; looks for a cure for his ailment.

The pain throbs again to remind him it will be with him until he finds,

his so called cure.

Searches upon searches, and no one is up to the task of hunting with a dying stalker.

His wound is now making him weaker.

He needs a strength. He needs one to call to be his reliance.

Then one steps out of the underbrush and says they are up to the task of being his strength.

Hesitantly he agrees to the unbelievable proclamation.

He now searches, seeks, and stalks with another.

They stalk and somewhat kill their prey as one.

The partnership was becoming more of a relationship, or so thought the deluded tiger.

The wound seemed mended now, and emotions aren't being lost to the wind.

One fatal date, under the calming breeze of night, the Tiger was again betrayed.

This one was supposed to be his strength, but just left him without a word.

This one must be afraid of him or afraid of what will happen after that one opens up

Once again, to another.

The wound is once again opened, and he does not care.

The pain he feels will be his strength, his only relationship.

From now to the end of his eternity, the pain will be with him.

He will no more try to find one to mend his wound.

Let all his emotions be lost to the wind.

It matters not.

For he knows he will die by himself, forgotten.

He knows he will die,

Alone as a Wounded Tiger.

DRAGON FLOWER

Vexation....Dragon Flower?
Poisonous with demonic power?
No, but she possesses hearts
as though she were an ancient evil.
Her visage weakens wills,
Men's courage departs, and their souls
become fragile and feeble.
Vexation....Dragon Flower?
Enchantress from the darkside,
Poised... to devour?
Make mindless your victims, by
Giving glimpses of where
The damned reside?
Your fragrance o flower,
Is deadly venom to man.
Dragon Flower, do you
bloom again,
Into death?

DRAGON FLOWER II: BLOOMING

The whole world
Is in turmoil at your beauty,
Dragon Flower.
Who are you?
What are you?
Why does merely your appearance,
Devour?
Fiend, Enchantress?
No, you are a vexation.
Your beauty stuns
At first glance.
It surrounds, without
Giving a chance.
Then skewers,
With mesmeric elation!

A TIME BEFORE

I mourn for my wife.
Not because she died, but
Because I never had one in life.
Many chances to be married.
Yet, the old man manipulations,
Made it, an unwanted
Weight to carry.
Now younger and wiser
Is my song.
But the irony is clear.
All those past chances
Are gone.
So, I take chance's place.
To remove the pain,
From my heart's surface.
All the invisible tears
For my wife have been cried.
Even as chance I still mourn.
For emptied is my heart.
It feels cold inside.
I only met my wife's qualities.
They are to teasing and tormenting,
To embody one body.
A weak chance am I.
I don't have the power,
To make her qualities comply.
So God fills my space.
And let's me know,

I must wait on his time and grace.
Then the embodiment will
Appear before my eyes.
Me and she will get married,
And real tears I will cry...maybe.

WINE OF TEARS

Thirsts of pain quenched with a wine of tears.
This ancient nectar pours in times of bravery,
And in times of fears.
A salty elixir, which is bitter to some, and
Others it's sweet.
It is used to say farewell, and at times, it is
Used to greet.
But is it good to indulge in this unusual champagne?
Some become famous, while others fall in shame.
Even those who take the wine as food for thought.
May end with a heaven lost, and a hell bought.
No, such a thing cannot be so important, so deadly.
Yes, for to dwell on it long enough, would be like playing
Your own mortality medley.
The boot liquor is stored in a cellar, behind human eyes.
Only a few can control their emotional gears.
It is automatically released for most when they cry.
This potentially potent potion,
Known as the wine of tears.

CHIDHOOD SWEETHEART

Her beauty was timeless even at our early age.
She always left me flustered,
But my libido was left enraged.
I had no evil intentions towards her.
My heart was softened, maybe stirred.
Everytime I would encounter
This heart rejuvenator.
I felt as though there was a slight chance for me.
If not at that time, then maybe later.
A love to me, God would decree.
Sad, a warrior on the brink of going mad.
Over an abundant convenience, he
Could only wish to have.
He did have this convenience sometime
In the dateless past. The only thing remaining,
Of this convenience, is the scene
His subconscious could grasp.
A pitiful scene, drenched with
The last drops of his tears. The last
Bit of his emotions buried deep
Within the years.
To draw forth those images makes his sad.
To remember an emotionless man,
Who was only a lad.
Or maybe, too much emotions numbed his brain.
Or maybe, too much sensitivity almost
Drove him insane.
But yet, the one sure thing he remembers is the pain.

A close friend in those times, who afflicted,
But also soothed his brain.
Flickers and flashes of love, flough the fearless fighter's mind.
Mere moments of mutilated memorabilia, are
The only traces of love he could find.
Yet seeing her, stirs something he truly thought was lost.
Now he thinks, that maybe memory and love signals,
are getting crossed.
Or possibly, memories of love uncovered,
That was covered with mental block moss.
Nevertheless, she is beautiful beyond her years.
In the past it the number of their earthly years,
That perhaps made them scared. He was aware
That God must have ordained her, over and eternity ago.
To be an example of an angel to mere mortals below.

I REALIZE

I realize you are the only one for me.
Sometimes during the day,
You infest my thoughts.
The times with you,
were the times
I was most happy.
Yet when we broke up,
The time I was most lost.

I SEE YOU

I see you in my dreams.
In the day and in the night.
You are outside of time's seams.
But brought to earth, so we can unite.

I see you in my mind.
A vision from God Almighty.
You are so lovely and so kind.
An immortal being in the expanse of eternity.

I see you in my heart.
A ray of light warming the cold abyss.
You made the frozen blood pump again start.
Then become filled with pure bliss.

I see you in my soul.
An image engrained before all things.
Before the age of fire, and the realm of cold.
Your beauty will eternally be captivating.

YES I REMEMBER, I REMEMBER

Yes I remember, I remember.
You were as beautiful as the sun in the morning.
Yes I remember, I remember.
In my cold heart you placed a kind warming.
I found something of me in you.
And you found traces of yourself in me too.
That's what attracted us to each other
And why our love grew.
But one fatal day
Into the wind the relationship blew.
Still now I can see your hair.
Like strings of honey enticing to any bear.
Yes, I recall your curvaceous thighs.
And the angel like glimmer of your pretty eyes.
What happened to us?
Why did we let the bonding slip away?
The relationship was certainly a plus.
But foolish will, allowed it to be cast astray.
Flashbacks of times you laughed and times you cried.
Loves were born, but ours had died.
At moments, just staring at each other with no words,
Because our tongues were tied.
We left each other to carry on.
The feelings are still here,
But in different directions we have gone.
Wanted and unwanted memories.
Spread over mind fields that are vast.
It was so beautiful, that sometimes

We just have to dwell in the past.
Yes I remember, I remember.
I will up to my death.
Yes I remember, I remember.
Even then, I will not soon forget.

FINALE OF THE FURY

Into the cold silence, the rider of the pale horse did trot. All was quiet. The total feeling was gone. Like it
was for naught. He was victorious. The urge was dead. Like an uneasy calm, before an expected storm.
Then all of a sudden, a loud sound was heard. It was followed by an undefined shriek. The likes of which
No mortal has ever heard. He raised his guard and prepared for the worse. The loud sound was now
many loud sounds. It seemed to not only fill the skies, but also, the very ground. It sounded like a
galloping horse to the strong and the weak. As the gallop got closer, so did the shriek. The master of
the death urge was returning for revenge. Now he must deal with death himself. On darkness he must
binge. That would be the ultimate solution to the death urge, even the finale of the fury. Death came
with a savage rage, on an evil stead. But where was the shriek coming from? Like a blood thirsty
vampire, the death urge was back to end the unfinished battle. No time to run and cower. The urge was
back with an irresistible power. The next time it leaves, it plans to take him with it. The last time, was
just some twisted trial, with all the gadgets and gidgets. It was to judge if he had too much good to offer
the world. He had more than too much, so the verdict was the death penalty, he had to die. When the
verdict was reached last time, they tried to kill him. Yet, he had enough strength to defeat them. This

time the strength is gone. The fourth horseman is smart to the fact, and so is the death urge. He has no

real resistance and he knows it. Waning skill reflect it. Life offers to help, but is instantly rejected. He

remembers the kind of help that life offers. Life indirectly offers death. Suddenly, the finale of the fury,

truly begins. The walls in his mind are starting to close in on him. He has not the inner strength to stop

those walls anymore. Pain pours on the poor. He is losing the battle. This cannot be. He is the

invulnerable. He cannot, will not lose. But maybe death is the solution. Life or death? It is a question

which others have answered, but has to be answered by him. He already knows the verdict. Will he

accept death without a fight or will he conceive the inevitable. Relentless attempts and hell bond efforts

to tear the invulnerable's mind. What or who has been keeping him holding on to life? He knows and so

does that person. Could the feelings of another mean so much to him, to keep him by the thread of life?

He is an intellectual prodigy to the end of his awesome sanity, and the beginning of a new even more

astounding madness. One person alone is the barrier that is stopping him from falling into the darkness.

Maybe this one could be his strength. Maybe he is too sentimental. Foolish attempts to call, cry to the

person for help. In those attempts he looked crazed, so the person wanted nothing to do with a

madman. He tried to make that one understand, but appeared even more twisted. The barrier was gone, or the force field was lifted. Nothing was to keep him from falling. The death urge is now like an

unstoppable force that cannot be denied. He knows he must find a reliable source on which to feed on,

or he will be overcome by this dark power. Still he cannot. No one is there to help him. There is one who

thinks he is just crazy. Puzzling thoughts, about what made the death urge arise again. What caused the

resurrection of this evil spawn? He alone is the answer. He is the one who summoned the death urge

and its creator to take him on their journey from which there is no return. He had the answer to

question. Life or Death? Now he is having second thoughts but knows in the end he will stick to his first

choice. In the past, anyone who summoned the death urge has been slain, literally killed by their own

hands. The last encounter, the urge of death was slain, smothered by an indomitable person. It was

really a Divine intervention. This time it is different, he is alone. Everything to lose and nothing to gain.

It does not matter, he does not care. Yet, the finale of the fury is magnificent. Explosions of violence,

bursts of rage, storms of wrath, plumage the invulnerable's body. The sheer fire of the fury is like a kind

of burning and boiling within his brain. A fuming anger, foaming fiercely, fretfully flushed with a fantastic

fuel and a flaring froth, fully intent on the invulnerable's fall. The fury is upon him ferociously fast. As it's

name sake, it's attack is sudden and swift. He is under siege by a savage sin, striking spitefully and sullenly. The phrase, "death has many faces," ring on in his mind. He now realizes the rider of the pale

horse is never seen when he fights the death urge. It is obvious. He curses himself for the fool he is. The

death urge is the grim reaper in his most successful form. Could he go down in history as one of the few

that has denied death it's desire for destruction? With that thought, a jolt of energy surges through his

soul. He thought he was alone, but the highest power intervened once again in answer to his silent cries

for help. Along with his rejuvenated power, he also has his resurrected beliefs. He defended and

attacked with those beliefs. The attack is feeble and death simply laughed at his attempts. Those beliefs

are always uses as a last resort. They are now low and weak because of misuse by backsliders. Death

counters with a blow full of memories, hardships and life. He channels that blow into a bolt of

irresistible force that can rend an irreparable mortal wound in the invulnerable. He is the last of his

kind. Last of a race of invulnerables. He can hear them calling to him from beyond. They wait for him to

join them. Any regular person would have already been destroyed by the robber of life. He is made of

tougher stuff. He is, or at least he was the invulnerable. For he is one struck with the death blow and he

is dying. The odds belonged to the one the Valkyries ride with. If he does not find some kind of weapon,

some kind of strength, he will perish in the finale of the fury. Then unable to withstand the relentless

pummeling by the forth horseman, he falls. He feels as though his hands were tied, as he looked from
his know kneeling position. The rider of the pale horse was holding a black double-edged axe. He could
do nothing or wanted to do nothing. Just as the axe struck, all went dark and all was quiet. Was he one
more stepping stone in death's desire for destruction? Did the grim reaper claim another soul? He hears
laughter as he contemplates many questions. The laughter became louder as he started to open his
eyes. When his eyes were fully open, he looked around but no one was there. It seemed like he was in a
cemetery. He feared for the worse as he backed up. He bumped into a tombstone by a grave which
seemed freshly filled. As he looked at the epitaph, he feared for the worse. It read: Here lies the corpse
of an invulnerable man. Who took a gamble and lost the bet. Killed by the death urge, one of the many
faces of the pale horse rider. One of the many faces of death."

HERMOSA

I hear your song when you smile at me.
It's like an enticing exotic melody.
Drawing me closer is this lullaby
Which is so moving it brings tears to my eyes.

The very adjective of your name, describes a melody
That is soft and sensuously sweet.
I heard it when we first kissed.
Like hearing a canary, while accomplishing
A tremendous feat.

A single word, played over and over in my mind without fail.
A simple word, but when describing you, it must be
Described in detail.
Your smile is angelic to a form
Of almost perfection.
Visuals of your image batter my mind constantly.
Like a shadow in sunlight, no dream's tainted scenery.
Your name's the same as a wealthy ancient empire.
But you are your own gold, and all sensible men's desire.
A delight to the senses warm and bright.
Sometimes I prefer you than the sunlight.
In my heart, feelings I didn't think were still there.
You've caused some of them to arise and reappear.
You are the meaning of this word.

What more can be said.
To disagree would be totally absurd.
Because your inner and outer beauty is like food,
Which to the starving must be fed.

SPECIAL TIME

That special time in the winter season.
That overcomes the hardened heart without reason.
That makes a man strengthen ties and forget treason.
And causes childhood emotions buried in a mind to arise.

Presents presented.
No sorrow rented.
Christian views cemented.
And happiness consistent, but no surprise.

Homemade bread along with winks and smiles.
Extends this holiday's mesmerizing all the while.
Melodies in the air add to goodness and discourages any
guile.
Curses spat at the midnight chimes that announces a new
day to rise.

No one sane wants this day to end.
As they assure themselves along with a friend.
Christmas will last forever, but time can't fully mend.
The beginning of itself when man was presented
In Bethlehem with his greatest prize.

WHO KNOWS

No pricelessness in a life after it dies.
Would those who believe this be considered simple or wise?
On a beach, is there significance about one missing grain of sand?
Is death just a new beginning in a new land?
Does the death of life change a generation's destiny?
Or does it just leave more room in the world for you or me?
Does a life have the same value when it's cold in a grave?
Or is a dead life worth more, and less harder to forget or waive?
Should a tear be shed for a life that is dead?
Should a life be stunted, when maybe a corpse has a new life ahead?
Would it be better to be dead or be alive?
Should we seek for the urge's master or for our ultimate goals should we strive?
But certainly, there is morbidity in humanity.
And of course a kind of serenity in mortality.
Yet, that is what makes living have a flare.
And what causes death to in a person's heart, put a scare.
Any pricelessness in a life after it dies?
No one fully knows.
The total picture is seen through God's eyes.

DARK ROOM

Bleakness tempered with cold.
Poison is one path.
Occupants from the young to the very old.
Awaiting heavenly bliss or hellish wrath.
Thoughts turned.
Now paradox with precept.
Earthly ways spurned.
While voices confessed and wept.
Vehemently passionless
Mild fervents.
Indifferent fierceness.
Eternal life is it's only present.
Good and evil persons must enter the hazy gloom.
And the same persons must also leave.
All given chances to change in life,
And avoid the negative path outside of the dark room.
Which is too horrible even to conceive.

MORTAL ANGEL

Is there such a thing as a mortal angel?
Why then is her visage heavenly?
For her, any man would bid his senses farewell.
And with the rest of his life, try
To make her a perfect medley.
Is there such a thing as a mortal angel?
I think she would be describes as one.
Her beauty is like a divine spell,
And her personality is like a another one.
Is there such a thing as a mortal angel?
She is the proof to answer that question.
No other woman is her parallel.
No man has ever denied her Celestial disposition.
Is there such a thing as a mortal angel?
Maybe no and maybe yes.
One answer deals with heaven and the other with hell.
In other words, for some she could curse and for others
She could bless.

A TASTE OF BLOOD

She went for the jugular and struck blood.
I realized it as my body hit the floor with a thud.
She stood over me smiling and smirking.
I felt beside us as if a dark force was lurking.
Even I the invincible had to scream.
As I noticed her eyes quickly flash with a crimson gleam.
I crawled backwards away from her and touched my neck.
Blood was running like water, and I thought it was just a little peck.
She walked after me with her smile getting wider and wider.
As I saw drops of blood drip from fangs that protruded her smile.
I was certain the dark force was the pale horse rider.
I struggled to my feet while conserving my fleeting breaths.
Even though it seemed like I was about to die,
It felt as though I already died a thousand deaths.
The pain was so terrible I had to touch my neck again.
The bleeding has stopped and the wound vanished, not a mark remained.
Yet, it felt like the wound was larger and all my blood was gone.
It didn't matter, my greatest worry was if I would
Ever again see the dawn.
The nearest exit was a window that I ran too, to be set free.
When I climbed through, I glanced back,
And now saw her running after me.
Terror arose in my heart as I raced through the night.
Because I heard the gallop of hooves follow in my plight.

Terror was still in my heart, it didn't subside, and was persistent.
To survive, I had to devise the perfect plan, but it
Would have to be in an instant.
I tried to summon my senses, which had all fled away.
The only sense left, was a thought.
Which was live, live to see another day.
Naturally, I wanted to live, but that seemed like the perfect plan.
So into the night I went further, faster and faster I ran.
My heart was past terror, my brain past madness.
In this situation, there was no room for error,
And no room for childlike sadness.
While expecting the ensuing mutilation,
I wondered whatever happened to all
My invincible proclamations.
Before I thought of an answer, again I would feel her
Prodigious power.
A matchless blow knocked me face first to the ground.
It seemed I had reached the end of my final hour.
From behind, she picked me up at my sides,
As one might a child.
Her hot breathing was getting closer to my neck.
I knew it again would be defiled.
I knew for sure, when I felt the stabbing pain.
Because fangs again had punctured my jugular vein.
I got weaker by the moment, but only then did i
Begin to fight.
She laughed, and flung me against a tree.
Yes, even more mocking, my miserable mortal might.
Slamming into the tree cleared my mind

Of any resistance.
I waited patiently for the end, until I saw a light
Off in the distance.
A hope of help now, maybe even a small glimmer.
As I rushed towards it, passing around trees,
The light gave a blurry shimmer.
It was somehow eerie, but still it was something different
From the pain, and the day's eternal counter-part.
The light was coming from an open door of a house.
But when I entered, then déjà vu gripped my heart.
I knew this place, I was sure, I had been there before.
It was like the uneasy feeling before a storm.
Terror struck me, I had returned to the same place as before.
But before I reacted, there at the doorway was she.
With her changing image even more transformed.
Again she lunged at me. Nonchalantly I avoided the blow,
Kicking forward, striking her knee.
This made her angry, not like before.
Now she appeared more of fiendish ghoul
Claws curling, eyes flaring, fangs bared to kill,
But still I was cool.
Lies! No such thing as cool in the face of a demon.
I still couldn't understand, she was a beautiful lady.
How could this be, I just had to be dreaming.
I was trapped, no more escape. Nothing left
But to expire.
Not by any natural cause, but by a lady friend,
Who turned out to be a vampire.
I tried to move my limbs,
But they were cold and lifeless.
A solution came to me. To die knowing God again

Was my decision.
Maybe I could awake from this curse, maybe God
Would bless.
While closing my eyes waiting, I heard a scream.
I reopened my eyes, and she had vanished.
Plus the sun has risen.

ALL I SEE IS NIGHT

All I see is night.
Nothing else is in sight.
I wonder with the wisdom at my might.
What force has taken the daylight?

All I see is night.
With dirty demons daring dark deeds for the devil.
Presumptuous people feel themselves almighty,
In their everyday plight.
But don't realize they are nothing without God.
On the natural, and especially the supernatural level.

All I see is night.
Or Ragnarok after the second coming.
What mortal can withstand the indignant blight,
Or the cold death urge numbing?

All I see is night,
And now people wish for the dawn.
But they will be enveloped in horror and fright.
When they comprehend the dawn as they know it,
Is forevermore gone.

All I see is night,
And oncoming madness.
Men will beg, but the reaper won't administer the fatal bite.
They must repent, or stand alone to suffer
the night, the approaching darkness.

NO TITLE

Feelings that are gone overtime never change.
Only there are thoughts which can be considered deranged.
A new year is on the horizon.
A growing child of God, must never act
Like the devil denizen.
Praise God for friends and family.
This year, 2017. Is the year I fulfil one of
My Jehovah designed destinies.
Faith in God and the word is paramount in my life.
Only God can rescue one from all despair and strife.
So welcome, new period of 365 days.
God's miracles in my life will leave all shocked and amazed.

SHE RUNS

She runs, emitting her Siren Song.
Words aren't heard, but men run after
Wanting to sing along.
Her beauty is like music which cannot be resisted.
A bewitching lullaby which in men's minds is entwisted.

She runs, off into the night.
Allowing men to pursue in her perilous journey.
They are enticed to stray into her dark light,
To wander for an eternity.

She runs, trampling over feelings.
Men and Women dealt lethal blows from her
invisible dealings.
One smile can drive any man insane.
With love thoughts like plagues, decaying his brain.

She runs, with an aura that causes others
To have heavenly hallucinations.
They think they know her path,
But are in a state of obfuscation.

Some run after, trying to follow this pinnacle of female
desire.
But may run straight into the yearning pit of eternal fire.
She runs, but men, do not follow, women do not contest.
Let her run, don't fall prey to the harpy's harmony.

Leaving her alone, of all things to do is the best.
Pray your paths don't cross, or running at you from a distance,
Is she.

VISION IMAGE

The fragrance of your breath is like roses that grow in heaven.
If I had to hold my breath and take a guess
On a scale of one to ten, I would call you eleven.
You are exalted in an unsacrilegious sense.
Your aura of beauty is of such magnitude.
That the word to describe it, is simply immense.
I had a vison of you last night .
Your smile was as precious as gold,
And you were dressed in white.
Your hair was blowing and flowing in the wind.
Like a glowing magical wave,
That made me want to skywardly ascend.
You see, because you were already in the skies.
You were as brilliant as the moon,
And beauty was the color of your eyes.
For at that moment, I went insane.
I tried with everything in my power to just touch you.
But in hindrance I succeed, and in failure gain.
I knew my earthly mission would be completed.
If I could at least catch your glance.
As I watched you go upward in the skies, further and further.
I then realized there was no possible way I could have a chance.
Dream or vision, you were slipping away.
Yet, I was too determined, to let gravity get in my way.
All I could do was wish, hope and dream about
Being united with this gem.
The only thing I wanted was to catch your glance,

To at least touch your garment's hem.
I then jumped straight up, with all my might.
Miraculously I caught hold to a moonbeam,
A rope of light.
I climbed upward into a cloud.
In the distance you were dancing with stars,
And singing out loud.
I started to leap from cloud to cloud,
For the purpose of getting to you.
I wanted to know you, now for sure I knew.
The closer I came the further you went.
My hopes hit a crescendo, then hit a higher descent.
I was trying my hardest but getting nowhere fast.
As this moon goddess was slowly
Becoming a thing of my past.
Nothing left to do, so I gave one last try.
Gaining ground, and man I just wanted to cry.
As I came closer I noticed this goddess,
Weeping silver tears.
With those actions, she aroused my old fears.
I had one more cloud to go, I thought to myself.
As I came to a cloud.
Which was whiter than purest snow.
Finally, when I reached the cloud of the goddess.
I was hit by a beauty barrage.
As you looked my way I thought you weren't real,
Just only a heavenly mirage.
You then stretched out your arm which gave me
Incentive to get to you fast.

I took hold of your hand, I had finally
Reached you at long last.
I have reached you or so it seems.
For as we touched lips, I woke up from the dream.

IMAGINE

Cries of anguished souls, screaming their torment. Some of the damned

Maybe take refuge in scavengers bodies, doomed to feast on corpses to maintain

Their new life. Ghost dogs, vampires of the plain. Drag innocent souls screaming

Down to hell's flames. Demons guised as necromancers, perform miracles before human

Eyes. Feastings of mortal men, the spirits of melancholy glut to their fills literally this time.

Before the second return they were confined to only try the human mind and sometimes possess

A body. Mortals could always call on God to save them. The Lord has returned and has taken his

Followers. The Holy Spirit is also gone. Nothing but humans and evil, and also the indignation. Men still

Do not repent. Pain undenied, plagues bestowed, prophecy fulfilled at lightning speed. The easy

Way to escape the pain is to accept the number. Yes, feast on fellow man with fiends.

To think, a person will starve without the mark.

To think, a person will not drink without the mark.

To think, a person will have to die without the mark.

To think, a person will go to hell with the mark.

The human will is a dastardly thing, but certainly not up to starvation and thirst.

The irony is there, but not funny. The Great Tribulation will almost be unbearable and probably will be.

Imagine no guardian angels. Imagine seeing the vexations that have been trying us all our lives. Imagine
Combating these supernatural horrors without heavenly assistance. Chilling, just to imagine. Demons
That were bound since the fall, released to kill a third of mankind. The greatest earthquake ever.
Meteors, blood red moon, darkness, bowls of wrath, sores, blood rivers, poisoned drinking water, and
Still more. These are only the beginning of birth pains, until Jesus returns.

CLARA

A dear friend in two of my three junior high years.
Hurting, a seemingly needless invulnerable, nevertheless
You did lend an ear.
My pain eased for a while, but one day I noticed your tears.
Later, I found out, you were verbally abused by your peers.
Why did they hurt you Clara?

I turned my head in shame.
For the sake and popularity of my name.
Daily, I rode off into the sunset with my friends.
Daily, you were abused with slander, your scars could not mend.
Even I betrayed you Clara!

I rallied my fleeting courage and confronted you.
We talked for a few minutes, you called me a friend true and true.
When you said that to me I felt happy, but kind of sad.
Good friends was all; that made me agitated, but more so glad.
We had a good friendship Clara.

So what if you were poor.
So what if your mother couldn't afford to give you more.
You were as beautiful as the best.
Only thing, you were not as finely dressed as the rest.
It didn't matter Clara.
A shining star in the dark void of humanity.

Yours was the prototype of kind or sweet personalities.
The idiots only laughed because they were full of jealousy.
Someone they would never become or meet, a true lady.
The truth twist people Clara.

In the second year, they started to leave you alone.
You had more friends now, away it seemed our
Friendship had blown.
At the middle of the year, you came up to me an
Whispered in my ear.
"Wayne I remember and I still care."
I remember too Clara.

An eerie feeling struck me in school the next day.
As I noticed heads bowed, and your friends tears giving way.
In fifth hour, I heard that something terrible had happened
to you.
They told me you were dead, my anger grew, that couldn't
be true.
I thought it was more lies Clara.

But I had to believe it. I had to believe her.
I knew this friend, we both did. She was honest as you were.
I roared in rage, that day, no more work for Wayne C.
The entire class were in tears, they comforted each other,
But no one would dare confront me.
Smart!!

Some of the same that talked about you began to cry.
I wanted to vent my rage at those, but I only gave a sigh.
Later that evening I thought about you being gone.

We had to do the easiest, but hardest thing. Carry on.
True sweet Clara.

I thought you were consumed in flames, but when you
Saved your siblings, the smoke smothered you.
Now you're free from the pain; in heaven you have started
life anew.
Your smile above all is what I will miss.
Are you now captivating angels with your own happiness?
Are you Clara?

I look forward to meeting you again kind lady.
I will run up to you and give you a hug zealously.
Then all of your sweetness will come back to me.
All that was maybe faded in my memory.
Until then....Clara!!!

A WHIRL OF THOUGHT

A whirl of thought overtakes my battered mind,
As I lay in contemplation of your magnificence.
It sweeps me off to another dominion dominated by
The very essence of your existence.
In this I can live in ecstasy, nothing else is needed or wanted.
Sweet visions of beauty before my eyes are flaunted.
The whirl is now a soft wind, that I gladly float along in
I see large beautiful clouds parade by, in assorted
Colors like so many balloons.
Accompanied by melodies and tender tunes.
Then out my mind, out loud, emotions and feelings start to
spew.
Finally; in exact words is described my love for you.
After the words are heard, I feel a chilling cold.
I realized, in words, my total love for you can never be
completely told.
A love sick dream or a sick love theme.
Is this or is this not what it seems.
I pursued the thought of thinking of you and found a utopia
personified.
As I started to wake up it felt as though I cried.
That feeling was felt but no tears from my eyes fled.
Was it a miraculous occurrence or was it all in my head.
Or is this just another step in my mind's total decay.
I don't care, I don't want to care.
If I do I might find the daydream to be a horrible nightmare.
I premeditate and concentrate and then I close and reopen
my eyes.
I have returned to your dominion, and by this I am not
surprised.

FLIGHTS OF FANCY

Flights of Fancy is their plea.
As they are enthralled by life's tapestry.
But there still there is something they can't see.
There is a large rip in this scenery.

Flights of Fancy is what they want.
Yet unaware life is another way for death to taunt.
Spaces in time along with reckless tricks.
Thinking they're having fun, but rather receiving lethal licks.

Flights of Fancy is their cry.
To be carefree in an instant, in a blink of an eye.
Although getting what you want is not always the best.
Sometimes, it is better to be content with less.

Flights of Fancy is what they still scream.
Not sure that life is all of what it seems.
They want to frolic in a utopia dream.
But may end up flowing face down a cold, cold stream.

RETURN MANIPULATOR

Return Manipulator, new enemies doth summon thee.
Return with chariots of retribution and claim another victory.
They say tales were lies of power, lies of your mind supremacy.
Tear their thoughts, then throw the trash to therapy.
Your body is fuming with frustrations, as your mind is continually pressed.
Nightmares pollute your world, as you slip into a state of posttraumatic stress.
Blood trickles down your brow, while you realize,
Your best efforts compared to this slightest, are less.
Magnanimous, mysterious, matchless might, makes mere
Miserable mortals mutter madness.
He twists your very contemplations of attack or defense.
The Manipulator slays your sense,
Leaves you numb in nonsense. Or simply, extinguishes, execrable enemy essence.
Made addicted, drunk and dying, a guzzler of the river styx.
Your brain afflicted, while at you jugular, mind fangs puncture,
Flaming nails prick.
He smirks and you scream as he slams shut the lid of your cerebrum coffin,
With nothing else heard but a click.
Fluttering, furiously fashioned, fated failure, felt from fickled fix.
Your brain a blaze.
Your thoughts with haze.
Your soul is dazed.

Attacking anxiety assimulated as acid, assassinates, and amazed.

What is there left for you to do?

With your mind now mutilated, your very sense skewered through.

Nothing cause the Manipulator has cast a spell on you.

While weeping, witless wayfarers, wearily wonders, what, why, who.

Understand now, your best agitates, his least destroys.

Your so called powers are useless weapons of little soldier toys.

Past desperate seeking help from supernatural convoys.

Disguised darkness, deploys deadly decoys.

Crushed contemplations or emitted expectations.

Dared dares, dooms dawning devastations.

Fools fiercely flawed with frothing frustrations.

Old enemies join in with you new ones and still he

Is winning, the battle's tide does not pivot.

Witnesses of a slaying, he laughs while you all vomit.

All challengers ravaged, he sets no death limit.

Manipulator, mass murders many minds in mere minutes.

The situation is bleak, realizes the spineless weak.

You cowards and liars whose actions are oblique.

Bones dismembered, followed by a chilling shriek.

Be silent, stifle your screaming, the Manipulator now speaks:
"No more words are said

Men and women combatants brain dead.

Why did you summon me?

Why did you not let me rest in peace?

How idiotic can an idiot be?

You have no idea of the power that was unleashed.

Invisible pistols were cocked.
No matter if you contested, if your mind had doors locked.
I have entered anyway and left eternal scars, and
Immoveable mental blocks.
You are brain dead in a state of shock.
Like a vampire, but I only thirst for minds.
Like a werewolf, but your brain is what I only want to grind.
You tried to unbind the bind, but you were too tightly bound.
You fought the fight and lost, nothing else to be found.
I have quenched my thirst, and glut to my fill.
I never wanted to do it, but I missed the taste and
Thrill of a fresh mind kill.
As I glance behind and see the disembodied bodies.
A sick laughter in my mind reminds me of other gothic hobbies.
I must banish myself again, I must not cause anymore gloom.
Like the ones that just fell, others that don't heed the
Warnings of the tales, will meet certain doom.
I will pray to the Lord to forbid the demons from dancing on your tomb.
I defeated, but never intended that you would have to encounter
The dark room."

NO REASON

There is no reason nor theme to their sickened plot.
Why destroy a person because the same color as you they
are not?
Captives in a game, or prisoners in a charade.
A high penalty given, a high price was paid.
Bound in their own grip, snared in their mind made cell.
The same evil which promised them a new heaven,
Is the same evil that has bestowed them with hell.
The vermin was spawned in their brain from an early age.
It started to grow every year, and with it a twisted hatred,
A sickening rage?
What have they done? All they want is to establish
themselves,not
to take over and have the others on the run.
There is no reason for any of this mess.
It is nothing more than twisted morals and self- righteous
nonsense.
Some can be reached, while others are too far gone.
Some are the kings of the vermin, while some are just the
king's pawns.
To honestly hate another human, is to commit
Towards God a form of treason.
So the answer I have for the senseless racism and violence,
Is simply, No Reason!

TALE OF A GODDESS

I tell my tale of a goddess today.
She's a vision of beauty in every kind of way.
Like an angel, in this life she has a heavenly part.
She is so radiant, that her brilliance is beyond
The reach of art.

Of a goddess I want to tell my tale.
Against mere mortals her grace prevails.
Her smile alone make you fall in love.
Like some soothing spell that could only have
Come from the heavens above.

I tell my tale of a goddess,
And this is a tale which I must tell.
She is on a higher level and totally lovely as well.
This goddess is special because of her caring ways.
A beautiful woman I will remember for all of my days.

I told my tale of a goddess today,
With such an angelic form that made me simply want to sway.
I want to make her understand.
I love her with every ounce of my breath,
And will continue to do so even after my fall, even after my death.

EXAMPLE

You are so graceful, and so exquisite. Any man
Would forget everything else and simply want to love you.
Your unbridled radiance is like the brilliancy of the sun.
You are artistically enchanting like an unspotted rose in bloom.
Your magnificence is an enlightenment to my weary being.
The mere thought of your visage is like food for my ravenous soul.
It is as though your hair was woven be an assembly of archangels.
Your eyes are a phenomenon to behold.
Mysterious as a poet's imagination.
Vivid as a winter morning.
Someone like you just cannot be real.
To paint my imagination's picture of a woman of beauty.

DESCRIPTIONS

I would describe you as a song, a sweet lullaby.
Sung by a choir of angels,harmonizing together in the sky.
Yes, similar to a heavenly melody being whistled by the clouds.
You are a special tune hummed silently, but
Nevertheless heard out loud.
I would describe you as an exotic island breeze.
You put me at a relaxing calm and a soothing ease.
You give me a sense of refreshment like a breath of fresh air.
I want to close my eyes and then fly into your atmosphere.
I would describe you as the embodiment of beauty.
It's like certain special qualities were gathered and
Then combined to form thee.
The highest power caused them to arrange like
Some coalescence.
You are the result, a thing of beauty, or it's
Radiant essence.
I would describe you as a mystical fantasy.
So beautiful, that I think she cannot be.
Like a daydream, I wish that thought would come true.
I realize now that the daydream is what it seems,
And what it seems like is you.

GRAVE SONG

Words marking the end of a life. If we sing our grave song before our time, do we cease to be?

Contemplations by a youth. It means nothing but something. Sometimes an epitaph, sometimes

encouragement or wisdom to those that continue. He almost went before his time, dwelling on morbid

thoughts. Cold chills attacked him one day. His mind distorted by life already. Illness maybe. Devil's

foreplay. He rebuked it all in the name of the one God. Peace for a moment, all the chills went, but still it

felt as if his mind rose and played a few notes of his grave song. After; it descended back to the

forbidden corridors, the disturbed places. His mind was composing the music. The most powerful part of

it had started playing the song. But He did not think the domain untouchable would start it. He would

think that part of his mind would end it. Yet, that was not the case. It wasn't the time for him to sing his

grave song, not in the prime of his life. No matter what his mind thought. He started trying to change his

own mind about singing his life's last song. Memory memorials. The signs are always there, the

warnings. Do not sing your grave song before the appropriate time or else. Commoners say you can't die

by singing your grave song prematurely. As usual they are wrong. In this case, dead wrong. Idiots that

only agitate and think they battle with mind powers. Stupid they are and stupid they shall remain, for

they are lowly commoners. Even if you sing it before time
and don't die immediately, you will die sooner
that you expect. But after you die, your grave song is
forgotten. Not unless it is your epitaph. All but two
shall forget. God; .. and your tombstone!

THOUGHTS

There are so many words that I can say.
But I love you, are most descriptive of those words today.
I need, I want, and I love you so much.
That now I thirst, crave, and hunger for
Your slightest touch.
Can a person love so much to a state of obsession?
Then to a state of almost insanity?
To love until transformed to another realm,
A different reality?
The words I love you are magical, mystical,
Magnificently moving.
This elixir of words which are safe and sorry,
But not to mention soothing.
How simple, but so complex do these words seem.
With the intent to sway, detour off into a
World of a daydream.
So, I love you were the words I used this day.
So, for now that is what I have to say.
So, some other time I will describe those
Words, in some other way.

DEATH URGE 1986

His life is crushed, feelings shattered.
His emotions thrown to the four winds.
A bizarre change of events
A strange twist of fate to deal a mortal blow to the invulnerable.
This juggernaut to some miraculously survived,
Rejecting his own death urge with a barrage. Matchless blows
From his resurrected inner being. Again it strikes with a blood thirsty effort.
It lunges to the throat of its victim,
Hapless attempts, defense and counter exceed or recede.
This invisible foe with a visible cause.
Now drunk with the nectar of death, the foe
Searches, seeks for that one.
These two have met before with strategies and tragedies,
With juggernaut the victor.
Triumphant the victory, but scars of the fiendish onslaught
Ravage the invulnerable. No one living can withstand such a fury,
Twice in an eternity. But would this one be considered alive?
If your deepest thoughts were repelled or disregarded by
Jealous lesser ones.
New views, other reviews and twisted clues.
To a heart that is shattered into a broken puzzle. The pieces
Reassembled with parts missing or cold as a void or vacuum.
It is different, but familiar in some awkward ungainly fashion.
Now the feelings are produced in the mind not the heart.

Now feelings are thoughts, thought up by the mind.
Life itself joins in the battle
A needed friend or unwanted foe?
It is loyal for a short span, but lands a prodigious blow.
The likes of which no person has ever felt.
More painful than a blow from the legendary Excaliber.
Life betrays as well as reminds you.
It was itself who caused the problem, and who is the solution.
Your emotions gone, replaced with; contemplated plans,
Researched schemes, and step by step procedures.
Left behind is a carcass, a corpse of a man.
The fury comes, no matter alive or dead in any kind of
sense.
It comes. Advantage or disadvantage. For the so called
Invulnerable, it is the latter. He still has not recovered,
Or will not ever fully recover from the first attack.
This words, "Life is not the solution," ring in his mind.
His own death urge rises again, recovered from matchless
blows.
It beckons to him, calls forth from His own decaying inner
being.
Yes, decaying, decomposing and rotting.
He realizes the second fury as begun.
This time, it tries him through his own battle scarred mind.
His dream, unconscious reality is defeating his inner being.
It..What was or maybe who is this it?
This invisible for who tries to defeat juggernaut.
They have fought many insignificant battles,
And one which can be described simply as fury.
Illusive as a ninja, mysterious as the pyramids.
This foe is the one foe who can destroy, kill,

Plumage without lifting a finger. But still who or what is he.
Blood runs freely shining like a light far out from a lighthouse.
This time the invulnerable lives up to his name.
Real or imagined, the foe has been conquered.
But is it defeat or victory? Illusions of humanity before his eyes.
Dreams cannot be this sour. An unusual formality of reality.
This opponent nurses from and endless supply of strength.
Invisible but clear as he is.
While the invulnerable has no source to replenish his waning might.
Life is no solution, what exactly does it mean?
These words he hears in his mind. The shadow of
The fourth horseman can be felt as he laughs in cold silence.
It would be so easy to stop those words in his mind from
Reappearing. That same juggernaut to some contemplates a
Question. Life or Death? It is a question with so much unbelieved
Importance that it means nothing. Suddenly in the dead of this
Unearthly like silence, he screams as he does is enough to send
A chill down the spine of the buried. He realizes he has not won.
He has conquered nothing but himself. This foe is to the climax
Of its attack. He strikes forth, but nothing is there to meet the blow.
Once it was said he could not be intimidated. Why does he now
Cringe and cower? The foe has tasted death nectar and i

Is now addicted. He wants to indulge. The tide of battle
Drastically changes to the relentless foe. Levels have been ventured
That cannot be mentioned. Everything to love and everything to gain.
The invulnerable has thoughts an fears which cry to him, run.
But he drives away those thoughts, curses those fears.
He counters with moves of a desperate man.
Even the foe is amazed at this one's courage.
But is it really courage or simply stupidity? Smoke if intensity
Rises as eternity sits in the waiting and death waits for a reward
In any outcome. The foe in the heat of the confrontation reveals itself.
It is the accursed death urge that is in all of us. This battle is more
Than a conflict, a decision to make. The question, Life or Death?
A choice must be made. The battle rages on. He cries out
In the cold silence, but then remembers who is there.
The master of the death urge. The one mortals have written
About since the beginning of infinity. He sits there on a pale horse,
Just waiting. You disregard him as he continues his battle.
You cry out to God, but hear no reply. But you feel replenished
With strength enough to win your battle. To defeat that ancient foe.
Finally, the fury has left you, but is that the truth or a lie.
For now it really does not matter. The foe has been defeated.
The death urge has been smothered. The rider of the pale horse,

The fourth horsemen trots off into the cold silence, the deadly cold silence.

He is safe for now, but knows one day, he will hear the sounds of

his worst enemy. The sounds of his own death urge.

AMONG FLESH

Among flesh...

You have been there like no other.

Even more than friend, father, sister or brother.

Among flesh..

You have always been there to help us through.

With your love, wisdom, and guidance,

there wasn't anything we couldn't do.

Among flesh..

We cried, "Happy mother's day!"

Untill the words reached the heavens,

and the angels themselves began to sway.

Among flesh...

We carried ourselves with a sense of morality

and justice.

Because it was you who instilled the foundation

of God within us.

So beyond the day for mother's we recognized,

our eternal love for you will continue,

beyond the flesh, when all else has died.

UNWORTHY OR WORTHY

To be untrustworthy or unworthy?

It's the same difference.

To wrap betrayal in a cloak of honesty.

Does that give full clearance?

To shed the emotions,

that were built for many years.

To destroy an otherwordly bond,

and not cry one tear.

In fact, a nervous smile was present.

With bloody fangs protruding through,

to fill a cracked heart with resent.

Beyond the betrayal,

it's the reeking time, that's

now precious waste.

Below the vail,

are crimson lies,

that are toxic to the taste.

Sadly, foreseen now,

was future in the past.

A untrustworthy, and

an anointed soul together,

would never last.

TORMENT AND SORROW

When the mental heart breaking,

blends with a physical heart aching.

It's like a symphony of catastrophe

and time.

Which mix into an ungodly concoction,

to drive anyone to the brink of being out

of their mind.

The memories haunt, yet tare at your soul.

Vivid pictures gleam but still fool's gold.

For such a cohesive past,

to not have a trace in the present.

The symbiosis of two, broken into halves.

Makes pain of the two felt by one,

never ever pleasant.

Scream to heaven "Away vile curse of torment and sorrow!"

Gambling that pain from betrayal will ease from a tomorrow.

Alone again seems to be a recurring theme.

With tears as soothing friends and

unearthly whispers as frightening dreams.

Waking still the hurt inside.

Damage more than done to not just your soul,

but to your indomitable pride.

A wounded tiger still hunts,

just more cautiously.

God alone can help to find the parody.

Or better yet, the clarity needed to continue.

To look through hurt and pain,

is not the only view.

Core morality believes,

Divinity will send the right one.

Together you will shine beyond,

what human thoughts can conceive.

Then be more radiant than a sun!

LETTING GO(PHASES)

(Phase 1)
Letting Go!

The words are easier said than done.

Like acknowledging the sunshine, while denying the sun.

Yet, sometimes, sunshine can shine too bright.

And have you craving the dark, yes have you craving the night.

At first you just feel pain.

It's an aching in your heart, mixed with a numbing of the brain.

Next, is a mockery of the past, that haunts to almost drive you insane.

In certain relationships, points of no return must be wrought.

Your soul calls out, and your future is besought.

By Divine Providence, the words are whispered, "Let Go!"

God allows the words to echo, so you will know.

The chasm in your heart will be filled one day.

If you continue on the path, and don't backtrack or stray.

Even if the path isn't clear or visible for you.

Moving forward with faith is the best thing to do.

(Phase 2)

Letting Go! Letting Go!

Like a symphony on your mind.

Musical, but inebriating as if, drinking too much wine.

Memories flog, like a fiasco of flames.

Images of certain faces bite, like a disturbed ant hill,

in the veins.

Letting Go! Letting Go!

These syllables flow and smoothly glide.

From words, to music, to drink, or even numbers.

Like the digit eight on its side.

Representing an eternity, that can be changed by your selection.

You are not to be controlled by a dependency or the very person.

Letting Go! Letting Go!

Fractured but never finished.

Allow your heart time, to knit and mend.

The wickedness will finally feel banished.

In the birth of a new beginning, from a relationship's end.

REMORSE IS TORTURE

Sweet memories,

that turn into something bitter.

Damned reasonings,

seem to be covered with glitter.

Kicking yourself

over taking the logical path.

Add to the pain,

and the mental bloodbath.

The rut is the monotony,

and the monotony is the rut.

Locked in life on a leash,

like a leech, longing for lust.

Ideal circumstances,

of thoughts long eclipsed by time.

Take root beyond reach,
With a symphony, of tears and

Rhyme.

IN GLORY NOW

You're in glory now.
Receiving the end of your faith.
The angels sing a new song,
As you walk through heaven's gates.
The tide has turned and eternity smiles,
As you stand before the King.
Then you receive crowns worthwhile,
For your earthly ministries.
And not just for witnessing,
But the way you raised your family.
The moral center, the prayer warrior.
Peerless in our family's generation.
The way God moved when you fasted
And prayed, was truly an inspiration.
So rest anointed matriarch.
Your lessons we'll keep forever.
The love we feel is stronger now.
That's something death could not sever.

Printed in the United States
By Bookmasters